3/11
Snacks for
Design

Cupcakes

Shine

617 637
7154
Neyda

ISBN-13-9780999763216

Table Contents

Introduction

In this book we will be studying one of Paul's letters to the Ephesus Church. Paul wrote this from his Roman prison cell to encourage believers in their faith. Ephesus was a fledgling church that Paul had began in the midst of a city known for witchcraft and magical practices. God incredibly blessed this ministry and many turned their hearts toward Jesus and renounced their witchlike practices.

Paul encourages us in how to shine in our daily lives. It demonstrates to us who we are through Christ's actions on the cross. It displays our new identity and defines our new possessions as a follower of Jesus. It develops our newfound power and strength to live in our everyday world.

As I watch the news, the stories of more tragedies, troubles, and trials seem to be so overwhelming. I can easily slip into a valley of discouragement and despair. I want to crawl into my own small world and hide.

I will occasionally mutter under my breath, "God are you here? " "Do you see this? "Lord, what can I do about all this darkness? It appears so crushing." At that point I sense a gracious whisper in my soul assuring me, "The path to rid darkness is to shine more light. You can be a reflection of what I put in you! Let my light shine through you." He understood my spirit's sigh; I didn't even have to verbalize my inadequacies or fears yet, He stepped in with loving power and bolstered my confidence.

The Christ-followers in Ephesus were probably focused on the persecution they were receiving, but the book of Ephesians turned their attention toward their potential as children of Heaven and not children of this world. Paul spurs us as believers to use our gifts and talents to spread the Good News of Jesus.

Paul teaches the church that Christianity is for all men: Jews, Gentiles, male, female, bond, and free all are united in Christ. Through Christ we are brothers and sisters united in one goal- "to honor and glorify God".

> **EPHESIANS 1:3 (NLT)** "ALL PRAISE TO GOD, THE FATHER OF OUR LORD JESUS CHRIST, WHO HAS BLESSED US WITH EVERY SPIRITUAL BLESSINGS IN THE HEAVENLY REALMS BECAUSE WE ARE UNITED WITH CHRIST."

Ephesians is divided into two sections:

1. **Chapters 1-3 - Our relationship with God through Jesus. It focuses on our great calling, our identity, and our purpose.**
2. **Chapters 4-6 - Our responsibility as believers. It focuses on practical living instructions.**

When we are suffocating in the pools of despair and our feelings are sinking beneath the weight of worry, we can't see God's grace and glory available to us. We can't see the light above the trees. To extract ourselves from this defeated and crushed position we must focus on the powerful truth that we are freed and empowered by His grace. The truth of grace calls me to rise above troubles, the truth of grace calls me to soar above worries, and the truth of grace calls me to fly into the face of danger knowing He is with me. Romans 8:11 say that "The Spirit of God, who raised Jesus from the dead lives in you. And just as God raised Jesus from the dead, He will give life to your mortal bodies by this same Spirit living within you.") When I allow His grace, His power, His mercy to surge through me and pour into my bleak spaces then I will be able to shine.

The truth of grace calls me to rise above troubles, the truth of grace calls me to soar above worries, and the truth of grace calls me to fly into the face of danger knowing He is with me.

Darkness is the absence of light. The shadows of pain and the gloom of heartache shout their presence in the night. Fear sinks it's teeth in deeper. But then somebody lights a candle. A spark flickers and the flame grows, darkness runs and hides.

Have you seen the Harry Potter series? In the sixth there is a scene towards the end when evil organized appalling death. The task to fight the darkness ended in failure. Floating high above the perished hero is the dark character, the image in the clouds of a skull with a snake bulging from its mouth. The mark is a tremendous figure of intimidation. It taunts the resistance with the impregnable force of evil. In the next scene, the students of Hogwarts gather in horror and then Professor McGonagall raises her wand. The tip begins to glow expelling a small bit of light. Silently the others begin to do the same brave thing. They slowly lift their wands and the light begins to grow. When lights finally illuminate the space, the dark specter dissolves from within. This moment is a defiant, audacious move. Holding up the light in the deepest, darkest instant is amazingly scary. Isn't that why we find it so hard to do?

The light in me will shine as a beacon of His love to this dark world. We are to shine as a lighthouse radiating hope to a lost world that is floundering in a sea of their sin and shame. We are to shine like stars-exuding light and heat (did you know that every single star you see in the sky is brighter and bigger than our sun?). We are to shine like a torch-guiding people to Jesus. We do not have to produce the light ourselves, that gives me incredible peace- we just reflect His light. The light that He puts in us He deposited it at salvation! The Holy Spirit shines through us!

As today's light-bearers there is too much at stake to allow our lights to be vanquished. We do not have the privilege to sit under a bushel and hide our light. We cannot allow the light deposited by a gracious loving God to be hidden or quenched. He wants to show the world through us his peace and compassion. The light that shines is a picture of Jesus. Every time you care for someone you shine! People are desperate for this light! Shine bright for Jesus!

> **MATTHEW 5:14-16 (MSG)** "HERE'S ANOTHER WAY TO PUT IT: YOU'RE HERE TO BE LIGHT, BRINGING OUT THE GOD-COLORS IN THE WORLD. GOD IS NOT A SECRET TO BE KEPT. WE'RE GOING PUBLIC WITH THIS, AS PUBLIC AS A CITY ON A HILL. IF I MAKE YOU LIGHT-BEARERS, YOU DON'T THINK I'M GOING TO HIDE YOU UNDER A BUCKET, DO YOU? I'M PUTTING YOU ON A LIGHT STAND- SHINE! KEEP OPEN HOUSE; BE GENEROUS WITH YOUR LIVES. BY OPENING UP TO OTHERS, YOU'LL PROMPT PEOPLE TO OPEN UP WITH GOD, THIS GENEROUS FATHER IN HEAVEN."

My purpose for this book is that you read the chapter for the week once daily. Let it soak in; permeate your soul. You can even select a verse that speaks to you and memorize it. But most importantly apply it! Ask yourself how can you take what you learn and make your world better?

Through all these pages think on your favorite dessert, for me is chocolate chip milkshakes, the ones that are homemade. The ones that are made with real chocolate chip cookies and good vanilla ice cream, not cheap ice cream. To really enjoy it, you deplete the cup slowly, savoring each sip, enjoying every flavor. I like to completely drain my shake; in fact, I like to scoop the crumbs off the bottom. I don't mind making a mess when it's really good. For the next few weeks we are going to dive into our study like it's your favorite dessert! We are going to slowly allow the word to soak into our lives and saturate our being! Allow God to make a mess in your life and change some things around!

Notes

Shine

Chapter 1: Ephesians 1

Our Possessions in Christ

Our Possessions ~ in Christ ~

When we receive the gift of salvation we receive all the benefits that come with it. We must accept that Jesus died on the cross to pay for all of our sins past, present and future, and use acknowledge that without his payment we cannot earn our way to Heaven. The Bible says at that moment we receive "eternal life". We can forever be content and rest in His promises of Heaven and the potential that salvation brings. The Bible says the Holy Spirit lives inside of us at the moment of salvation, which enables us to live courageously, compassionately, and contentedly.

When we forget what we have available we become spiritually defunct. This reminds me about a guy who won an all-inclusive vacation. He flew down to the Caribbean and went to this exotic resort but remained in his room eating the snacks he had packed. He didn't realize all-inclusive covered all the food and amenities. He didn't comprehend the scope of his gift. He missed out on a vacation of a lifetime that was already paid for. It was purchased, yet he didn't take advantage of all that was offered.

Or how about Henrietta Howland "Hetty" Green (née Robinson; November 21, 1834 – July 3, 1916) nicknamed the "Witch of Wall Street", was an American businesswoman and financier known as "the richest woman in America" during the Gilded Age.

Hetty Green's stinginess was legendary. It was said She never to turn on the heat or use hot water. She wore one old black dress and undergarments that she changed only after they had been worn out, did not wash her hands and rode in an old carriage. She ate mostly pies that cost fifteen cents. One tale claims that Hetty spent half a night searching her carriage for a lost stamp worth two cents. Another story of Hetty asserts that she instructed her laundress to wash only the dirtiest parts of her dresses (the hems) to save money on soap.

On July 3, 1916, Hetty Green died at age 81 at her son's New York City home. According to her longstanding "World's Greatest Miser" entry in the Guinness Book of World Records, she died of apoplexy after arguing with a maid over the virtues of skimmed milk. Estimates of her net worth ranged from $100 million to $200 million ($2.17 billion to $4.35 billion in 2016).

As believers we can be spiritual misers. We can go through life without taking advantage of what has already been paid for by the blood of Jesus. When we choose not to use our possessions in Christ, the riches of the Holy Spirit are left wasted. We live like paupers even when we hold the riches of the king. We live miserly by depriving ourselves of the blessings we have available and we deprive others because we cannot provide what we don't practice. However when we acknowledge our possessions and our privilege that we have in Christ we cannot only "endure hardships", but we can be "more than conquerors" (Romans 8:37). Remember knowledge without action is like fat (absolutely useless-unless you are like a sea mammal in the arctic circle); knowledge with action is muscle. God desires us to put our knowledge of the scripture to use by loving others and glorifying Him.

The book of Ephesians is like Cross-fit functional workouts. Functional workouts are a preparation of the body for daily life. We are learning and working it at the same time. Knowledge and application are walking hand-in-hand.

Paul penned Ephesians from prison in Rome in AD 64 to encourage and equip us as believers. Ephesus had been the center for worship of the goddess Diana (goddess of fertility). The temple Diana was considerate as one of the wonders of the world. Ephesus was a tremendous trade city it was called the gateway to Asia. The apostle Paul came to this area and preached salvation and freedom through Jesus. This stronghold of idolatry broke and a revival swept through the town. Paul wrote this book that was breathed by the Holy Spirit in celebration of the church. Paul celebrates our belonging to a body, our community of faith that transcends generations. Paul delves into the very core of what it is to be a Christian: the faith and the practice.

Remember the first three chapters reveal our position in Christ. We see His glorious gifts to us.

As we decide to let our light shine (the moment of salvation) we have to make sure we are completely and totally plugged up. The only way we can shine our light and make this dark world a brighter place is to stay closely connected to the power source.

A Maori proverb says, "Turn your face to the sun and the shadows fall behind you."

1. Selected (vs 1-6)

EPHESIANS 1:4 (NLT) " EVEN BEFORE HE MADE THE WORLD, GOD LOVED US AND CHOSE US IN CHRIST TO BE HOLY AND WITHOUT FAULT IN HIS EYES."

. . . .

Grace precedes peace.

. . . .

God has given us NEW life. He has already given us grace divine assistance for living (look at verse 2). But now He gives us strength to face problems. He gives us peace to withstand the chaos we deal with and changing circumstances. Did you notice the order He gives it to us? Grace precedes peace. Grace wipes out our sins; peace allows us to live in this world. In verse 3, we move to the blessings we have received. When we become Christians (ask Jesus to take away our sins) we become "in Christ". When we are in Christ, God sees Jesus when He looks at us. We stand clothed in His righteousness; we stand dressed in His goodness, covered in His sinless blood. Our position is perfect but our practice (our walk) is a process.

God chose us to be saved. In his sovereign plan, He desires everyone to receive the gift of salvation. Our responsibility is to offer salvation to all. Anyone can be saved when they repent of their sins and believe in Jesus Christ (Romans 10:9,13; John 3:16; 5:24). Some people read verse four and say why bother telling my friends? If God has already planned who is going to be saved and who isn't. The answer is we don't know. God is in control He is sovereign and we are not. We don't have a magic light bulb above some heads that glow to let us know they will accept Him. But we do have a mandate that tells us to go into the world and tell people about Him. In my opinion, I would rather err on the side of telling people about Him.

2. Saved (vs 7-12)

EPHESIANS 1:7 (NLT) "HE IS SO RICH IN KINDNESS AND GRACE THAT HE PURCHASED OUR FREEDOM WITH THE BLOOD OF HIS SON AND FORGAVE OUR SINS."

Before we came to Christ we were condemned by our sins and we were alienated from God. Christ's death offered us redemption, pardon and forgiveness. He forgave all of our sins and wiped the slate clean.

We are justified ("just as if I've never sinned") and sanctified (set apart for Him). We are freed from the bondage of guilt and shame; He redeemed us. He purchased us with a price the blood of His sinless Son. He paid for our sins with His blood and forgave our sins with His grace.

The Holy Spirit not only empowers us, He is God's pledge and commitment of God's redemption.

Verse 8 tells us He has shared His plans with us. He has given us wisdom and under-standing. He revealed His plans, the mystery of His will. His will is that people will know Him and live for Him.

3. Secure (vs 13-14)

When we accept the gift of eternal life from Jesus, accept Him as the payment for our sins; we become brothers and sisters in Christ with every believer; regardless of nationality, background or ethnicity. We are all "in Christ".

He also gave us the gift of the Holy Spirit as a guarantee. The indwelling Holy Spirit brands us as God's property (I Corinthians 6:19-20) and the Holy Spirit protects us (Ephesians 4:30). He is the "earnest" of our inheritance, the down payment for the things to come. The Holy Spirit not only empowers us, He is God's pledge and commitment of God's redemption. The Holy Spirit living inside of us helps us to fulfill His purpose for us. He secures us.

4. Supplication (vs 15-22)

Paul prays for the believers to develop spiritual muscles. He desired that they would grow in holiness, which is predicated by knowledge, knowing God more. This section of the chapter emphasizes that our work and the work of the Holy Spirit's goes hand-in-hand.

We study the Bible and He illuminates it. We willingly apply it and He provides opportunities.

In this section Paul acknowledges the believers strong faith; he sees them as steadfast and strong. Paul reiterates that faith, believes what God says about Himself, us and the rest of the world. Paul also thanked God for their love for His children. Paul prayed to God for the Ephesians that they might know the hope of their calling and that they would know that there is joy and fulfillment in living for Him. He also prayed for was knowledge of their richness of our inheritance. As Christ followers we are join-heirs with Christ (Romans 8:17). Additionally, Paul prayed for the Ephesians to know God's mighty power. The same power that resurrected Jesus from the grave lives inside us as believers. Simply put, we don't have to fight battles with our own strength. I'm not saying you will never fail or falter (remember your kids when they started walking they had to build their ability and confidence). Basically, the ability to succeed as Christians is already inside us. Sin doesn't have control of us. You are not the same person. You have a new heart; you have a new power.

Lessons Learned:

1. God chose me. He knew me and loved me in spite of my problems. (Galatians 1:15; Romans 8:29; Romans 11:2)

2. God redeemed me and forgave me. God looks at me as freed from sin (perfect) because his Son paid the price. (Psalm 49:7, 15; Galatians 4:4)

3. God empowers me with His Holy Spirit. He gives me the ability to accomplish what He has called me to do. (Acts 2:33; 1 Corinthians 2:4; Zechariah 4:6)

Group Questions:

1. In verse 1, Paul wrote about being "faithful in Christ" what do you think he meant by this? What are characteristics of one who is faithful to Christ?
(Exodus 20:3; Proverbs 3:12; 2 Chronicles 16:9; Matthew 25:21; Luke 16:10)
Trust, Honest

2. In verses 4-14 Paul lists the blessings we receive as Christians. List those and discuss how they affect us daily.
(John 3:15-16; Romans 6:23; Colossians 1:14; 2 Corinthians 5:18-20; Romans 5:9; Romans 8:1; 1 John 3:1-2; Romans 8:37-39; Galatians 3:14; John 15:4-8; Ephesians 2:7; Romans 15:17; Romans 12:4-5; Titus 2:13) Redemption, forgiveness, Holy Spirit, Eternal life

3. The same power that raised Jesus from the grave lives inside of me, but it takes faith to exercise that power. How can we use that power every moment?
(Ephesians 6:10, 18; Isaiah 11:2-5; 1Kings 19; 1 Corinthians 10:13)
- Identity in Jesus
- I am - Living in victory

4. Paul prayed that we would know Jesus. What does growing in our knowledge of Jesus require?
(2 Peter 1:2-11; Galatians 2:20; Colossians 3:16)
Live by faith in Jesus.
Worship + Word
Thankfulness

The great Scottish Bible expositor Alexander MacLaren once wrote: "We may have as much of God as we will. Christ puts the key of the treasure chamber into our hand, and bids us take all that we want. If a man is admitted into the bullion vault of a bank and told to help himself, and comes out with one cent, whose fault is it that he is poor?"

The Mount Morgan gold mine in Queensland, Australia, is one of the richest in the world. For many years, though, the original landowners lived in deep poverty on the mountain's barren surface. Even though the vast wealth was out-of-sight, it was beneath their feet all the time. Remember God saved us and supplied us. We must remember we are endowed with the immeasurable wealth of the Holy Spirit beyond all imagination.

Because of our love for Jesus and because of His enormous sacrifice for us, we get to honor Him and serve Him (that is the basis of our service). We are showing a lost and dying world a loving Father whose Spirit lives in us. We get to… not have to. When you love someone you want to exhibit your love, it is a natural outpouring. The reverse is true also; if you don't care for a person you are not willing to go out of your way to do some thing for them. Look at this verse. James 2:17 "Thus also faith by itself, if it does not have works, is dead." (NKJV) When we apply the grace given to us and live through the generosity of a holy, benevolent God, our world changes. We live out of the gift given to us. We are loved, we are chosen, and we are designed with a purpose!

Warren Weirsbe says in Be Rich, "We inherit the wealth by faith, we invest the wealth by works."
We are saved by Jesus by His death and resurrection; secured us by the Holy Spirit forever; and selected by God the Father for a special purpose.

Notes

Shine

Chapter 2: Ephesians 2

Our Position in Christ

Our **Position** ~ in Christ ~

EPHESIANS 2:4 -5 (NLT)"BUT GOD IS SO RICH IN MERCY AND HE LOVES US SO MUCH, THAT EVEN THOUGH WE WERE DEAD BECAUSE OF SIN, HE GAVE US LIFE WHEN HE RAISED CHRIST FROM THE DEAD. (IT IS ONLY BY GOD'S GRACE THAT YOU HAVE BEEN SAVED!)"

We have been raised from the dead; the Bible says we are like walking dead when we are living without Jesus, think Zombies, seriously- dead and decaying. We wonder with no purpose, aimless. But at the moment of salvation we receive new life. In Revelation 21:5 the Scripture states that He makes all things new; God doesn't just redeem us. He makes us new creations. Not only does He bring us back to life, He gives us a position and a purpose. We are seated on a throne. (Verse 1-10) We are no longer enemies but are now reconciled and set into the temple! (Verse 11-22) We can sometimes forget where we came from; but yet, He doesn't let us stay that way.

God's grace and mercy seem unbelievable: "too good to be true" at times. I read about an instant cake mix that was a big flop. The instructions said all you had to do was add water and bake. The company couldn't understand why it didn't sell—until their research discovered that the buying public felt uneasy about a mix that required only water. People thought it was too easy. So the company altered the formula and changed the recipe to call for adding water and an egg to the mix. The idea worked, and sales jumped dramatically.
Seriously, some people believe God's grace is literally out of the realms of possibility for them.

1. Our Past (vs 1-3)

Paul sums up the condition of lost men in one word: dead. To be dead is to be lifeless. To be dead makes you unable to help one. To be dead is to be absolutely powerless. To be dead is to be beyond hope (in the eyes of the world). The Bible refers to this "deadness" as a separation from Him. We need a resurrection! Remember God is the source and sustainer of life. All of us were born separated from God; we were born sinners (think about it- did you have to teach your kids to lie—did your baby scream when they were NOT hungry or wet? Mine did!)

In verse two we acknowledge our depravity. We conduct ourselves by our selfish desires, basically we all live according to what makes us feel good. We are innately self-centered. As a result, we were subject to the penalty of sin. We are sinners and we are dead— enough said! But hold on.

2. His Provision (vs 4-10)

Best words ever…look at the first two words in verse four "But God". His divine attributes of mercy (pardoning us- not giving us what we deserve) and grace (giving us what we don't deserve) walked in and revolutionized humankind. His love for us exhibited itself in grace and mercy. His agape, selfless love was so great that He didn't convict or condemn us; He placed all the burden of our sins on His spotless Son. He knew the payment for our sin had a to be an immaculate, sinless Savior. At the cost of His son's excruciating death He withheld our punishment. God placed His Son in human skin so we could be free from sin. He was born so we could be reborn. But hold on, keep reading, look at verse 6-8, not only were we forgiven -we are given a place of significance. He positioned us for greatness. He lavishly gifted us with a purpose. Wait another minute, in verse seven God tells us His grace will still be a force for our behalf "in future ages". His favor never diminishes and it continues.

EPHESIANS 2:8-9 (NLT) "GOD SAVED YOU BY HIS GRACE WHEN YOU BELIEVED. AND YOU CAN'T TAKE CREDIT FOR THIS; IT IS A GIFT FROM GOD. SALVATION IS NOT A REWARD FOR THE GOOD THINGS WE HAVE DONE, SO NONE OF US CAN BOAST ABOUT IT."

We are saved by faith to produce good works. Our good works does not save us; no one has enough goodness in them to outweigh the bad. Only Jesus, the Sinless Savior, was able to purchase our pardon and pay the price of sin. He completely irrevocably paid the price of our sin! When we believe Jesus satisfied the penalty and issued us new life, that's faith. However, we are not saved to sit and soak. We are called to make a difference in our community, in our country, in our world. Good works are the result of our salvation. We are so grateful and our lives are so changed that we desire others to know about Him, and to see the change He has made in our lives. God works in us and through us. The same resurrection power that raised Jesus from the dead and resurrected our dead lives resides inside of us. God gave us the Holy Spirit at the moment of salvation to equip us to do His will.

The fruit of the Spirit in our lives, when fully developed, should also permeate and saturate our surroundings.

The fruits of the spirit (Galatians 5:22-23) can be overwhelmingly evident. The fruit can be so ripe it oozes out! God worked for me, now. I can let Him work through me. There is one thing about ripe fruit that I have noticed it that saturates the senses. You smell ripe fruit- a mature mango sitting on a kitchen counter permeates the kitchen; the taste of that fully developed fruit is so vibrant! The fruit of the Spirit in our lives, when fully developed, should also permeate and overflow our surroundings.

Paul gently dealt with the alienation, the separation of the Gentiles from the Jews. The Jews and Gentiles harbored strong feelings of contempt for each other. (In Ephesus they only got along for business purposes.) The two groups had such animosity that there were many Jewish laws against Gentiles. For example, a Jewish person could not offer aid to a Gentile woman in childbirth even if she was in desperate need. To enter a Gentile house rendered a Jew ceremonial unclean. Marriage of a Jew to a Gentile was looked upon as the equivalent of death; they actually had a funeral service for the Jewish person who married the Gentile. The Jews really looked down on the Gentiles, calling them "uncircumcised." This insult was a reminder that the Gentiles were not in the covenant of Abraham and not included in the blessings promised to him. Although circumcision was a human work, it reflected a spiritual reality. The Gentiles were separated from Christ, hope and promise. But with Paul's writings that has now changed:

> EPHESIANS 2:13 (NLT) "BUT NOW IN CHRIST JESUS YOU WHO ONCE WERE FAR AWAY HAVE BEEN BROUGHT NEAR THROUGH THE BLOOD OF CHRIST"

Once they were separated from Christ; now they are united with him. Once they were excluded; now they are included. They have hope, and they have God, through the death of Jesus Christ. Christ died to break down walls.

Jesus removed the barriers. Because of Jesus walls are broken, racial hurdles removed. The blood of Jesus that covered our sins removes all skin color. The blood of Jesus unites us; it runs through our veins, it covers our sins.

In verse 15, we view wide-sweeping reform, Christ came to fulfill and abolish the Law, break down walls. The law held people out, Jesus brings them in close. Where the law built barriers, Jesus built bridges. The result is peace for all believers and access to the Father. We are no longer vagabonds wandering aimlessly with nowhere to rest our weary soul; we have a home in Christ Jesus.

The obstruction of hostility was the law, which had commandments and regulations separating Jew from Gentile. This law defined who was on which side of the barrier: it said who had the promises and who belonged to the people of God.

The law was eradicated once and for all. We are no longer slaves to the law; we are free under grace. When Jesus died on the cross, the veil in the Holy of Holies (the separation from priest to people) was torn, symbolizing open, free access to our loving Father. It symbolized reconciliation, restoration, and redemption with the Holy God. Jews and Gentiles are reconciled to God and each other through Jesus Christ.

Paul concludes with the picture of believers as foundational stones of a growing temple- His church, with Jesus as the cornerstone. Again Paul is conceptualizing unity. We are united in Christ, through Christ. We are one nation, a holy nation with our citizenship in heaven. We are one family. God is our father and we are brothers and sisters in Christ. We are one temple. He dwells in our hearts as those who have called him Lord. He calls our bodies the temple. (1 Corinthians 6:19-20) This is particularly interesting to both Jews and Gentiles. The Jews would picture Herod's temple and the Gentiles would think of the temple of Diana, both of which would be destroyed; but the temple of God lives forever because He is the cornerstone, the foundational stone for our future.

This chapter that started off with the description of dead, decaying Gentiles now ends with the Gentiles as cleansed pure, with Him living inside us. Grace rectified the chasm between God, and us but also between people groups. We are freed to glorify Him; our purpose shines in the temple (our modern day church) where together we reach more people for Jesus. God wants to build His church and to have fellowship among His people.

Chapter 2 takes us from death to life, from hostility to peace.

Lessons Learned:

1. Grace overpowers death. I am made alive in Christ. (Colossians 2:13; Romans 6:11; Romans 8:2)

2. I am saved by grace unto good works. My best works won't get me to heaven, only His grace, but I am saved to act like Him.
(James 2:26; James 3:13; Romans 11:6; Matthew 5:16)

3. Christ came to make peace. Peace between peoples, peace in the midst of a storm.
(Romans 12:18; Psalm 29:11; Isaiah 26:12; John 16:33)

Group Questions:

1. What is sin? How does it affect us? What does it mean to spiritually dead?
(1 John 1:8-10; Romans 3:23; James 4:17; Romans 6:23; Isaiah 59:2; John 15:5; Colossians 2:13)

2. What did God actually do when He saved us (2:4-10)?
(Romans 3:24; Romans 8:1-2; 1 Corinthians 1:30; 2 Corinthians 5:17-18; 2 Timothy 2:10)

3. Knowing we are "God's Handiwork", how should it affect our perspective on our purpose? What does that even mean?
(Ephesians 4:1-2; Psalm 139:13-14; 1 Corinthians 10:31; John 15:8)

4. What is a cornerstone and why do you think Jesus was referred to as the cornerstone? How can this apply to my life? What does it mean for me?
(1 Peter 2:7; Isaiah 28:16-17; Psalm 118:22-23; Matthew 7:24-27; Luke 6:47-49)

5. How can we bring reconciliation, peace to a world that hungers for it?
(James 1:19-20; Ephesians 4:32; John 14:27)

PEACE... the Ketchi Indians of Guatemala define peace as "quiet goodness". The Quechua Indians of Ecuador and Bolivia use a word for peace that means, "to sit down in one's heart". Peace in our relationships with God and others allows me to be settled, confident and determined.

The end of the chapter Paul discusses reconciliation. Jesus came to break all barriers.

According to **dictionary.com,** the simple definition of reconciliation is an act of reconciling, as when two former enemies agree to an amicable truce. Cambridge dictionary defines it as "process of making two people or groups of people friendly again after they have argued seriously or fought and kept apart from each other, or a situation in which this happens."
Reconciliation not only involves forgiveness, it goes a step further. Reconciliation includes the building of a relationship. Forgiveness is step one then you go the hard yards and reconstruct the connection.

The study conducted by the University of Michigan and partly funded by the National Institute of Mental Health, found young adults aged 18-44 were less likely to forgive others than middle aged adults (45-64) and older adults (65 and up). Younger adults were also less likely to believe God had forgiven them.

People who forgive reported decreased psychological distress, including fewer feelings of restlessness, hopelessness, and nervousness. Young adults who reported high levels of self-forgiveness were more likely to be satisfied with their lives. Older adults who reported high levels of forgiveness for others were more likely to report increased life satisfaction.

http://dailynews.yahoo.com, Journal of Adult Development 2001, December 31, 2001.

In his remarkable book, *No Future without Forgiveness*, Bishop Tutu, reflecting on his work with the South African Truth and Reconciliation Commission, writes:

"Forgiving and being reconciled are not about pretending that things are other than they are.
It is not patting one another on the back and turning a blind eye to the wrong.
True reconciliation exposes the awfulness, the abuse, the pain, the degradation, and the truth.
It could even sometimes make things worse.
It is a risky undertaking but in the end it is worthwhile, because in the end dealing with the real situation helps to bring real healing.

Spurious reconciliation can bring only spurious healing."

Jesus came to breathe life into crushed relationships. Jesus came to resurrect our dead and decaying hopes and dreams. He came to whisper words of truth when all you have heard are lies and innuendos. He came to shout encouragement as we forgive, and then as we leap into the frightening chasm of reconciliation He reveals His goodness and mercy as He travels with us.

Notes

Shine

Chapter 3: Ephesians 3

Our Prayer for Power

Our **Prayer** ~ for Power ~

EPHESIANS 3:14-16 (NLT) "WHEN I THINK OF ALL THIS, I FALL TO MY KNEES AND PRAY TO THE FATHER, THE CREATOR OF EVERYTHING IN HEAVEN AND ON EARTH. I PRAY THAT FROM HIS GLORIOUS, UNLIMITED RESOURCES HE WILL EMPOWER YOU WITH INNER STRENGTH THROUGH HIS SPIRIT."

Imagine the best dad you have known or heard about. Was he on TV? Did he cheer at the sports games really loud? Or maybe he was a character really encouraging when the kids were losing? Maybe the dad gave a kid an opportunity you never got? The thing about God is He is better than the best dad we could imagine, and He is not limited to humanity, He is limitless, He has no weaknesses, He doesn't get tired. He longs to give us every opportunity; He is cheering us on from Heaven! Even in the face of the impossibility, God will tell us that, through Him, all things are possible. In this chapter we delve into God's great love for us.

Chapter 3 opens with Paul speaking to the Gentiles. But let's review a minute: In chapter 1, we view what God made available for everyone and then chapter 2 delves more into what God accomplished for the Gentiles. Paul addresses our calling- what God has appointed us to do and how He will achieve this. Remember Paul was writing this from prison. Many theologians think that he was in prison due to the religious leaders of the day. They got ticked off because of what he was preaching; he ran into awful opposition in proclaiming that believing Gentiles enjoy equal rights and privileges same as the believing Jews. Paul preached the message that Jesus was the Savior for all mankind.

This new concept blindsided the Jewish nation, as in the Old Testament God primarily deals with the Jewish people. Most of the Old Testament spotlights Abraham and his descendants. When Jesus descended from heaven in form of a man He was rejected by the Jewish people. As a result, we are now living in what is called the "Church Age": Jews and Gentiles are on the same platform. God emphasizes He hungers to use the Church (all who are saved) to reach the world with the Good News! The church is not a conglomerate of people who crave religious activity; it is a vital instrument through which God is carrying out His plans. The Church is a breathing, living organism that grows, that feels, that cares, that hungers, that cries, that laughs. The Church is a force that is unequaled-the church is hope with skin. The Church is humility with unparalleled generosity; the church is the Bride of Christ. We live in the most exciting times for the Church; we are in the Age of Grace. Believers have the gift of the Holy Spirit; God gifted with power to accomplish the calling. His power aids us on our journey as we discover the road isn't straight and smooth, sometimes there are mountains to climb and adversaries to face. His infinite love, unfailing presence and immeasurable kindness escort us through the paths of life.

The gospel is simply Jesus died, was buried and rose again to give us life

1. Divine Discovery (v 1-13)

Paul was chosen by God to reveal the mystery of God's truth for His Church. The Bible calls them "Mysteries"- secrets and mysteries are only mystifying to the ones who don't know them. Remember God has always known His plans. The mystery of the Church is the specific purpose, which He assigned us. We are to be an international community, a body, an organism that grows and spreads by advancing the "Good News". Paul's job was like ours, to share the Gospel with unbelievers. The gospel is simply that Jesus died, was buried and rose again to give us life; He paid the penalty for our sins. Paul went further; he shared that salvation was offered to the Gentiles. Paul simply said we are joint-heirs with Christ (Romans 8:14-17). That concept is so hard to grasp. Spiritually speaking we get His divine nature, and we even look like Him (1 Peter 1:3-4). W have His rights. We are adopted into the family. Human birth defines our racial distinctions; but spiritual birth unites us as brothers and sisters and sons and daughters of the King.

That is the mystery- we as believers are all part of the Church to accomplish God's desire that no one goes to Hell.

In verse 8 and 9, Paul marveled at the grace God had gifted him with by allowing him, in spite of his personal past, to preach the good news. We, as Christians, can unite with Paul and preach the good news. "To Preach" in the Greek language, which the Bible is written is simply translated to "announce". We get to partner together and "preach" God's plan of salvation. In addition, we also receive the power to deliver the Good News, but look at verse 10… we are actually teaching the angels when we tell the redemption plan. Paul in verses 13-15 encourages us to not give up because he realizes that evil is all around and discouragement can creep in; he inspires us to persevere. Paul focuses our eyes toward our salvation, our hope of Heaven.

> **ISAIAH 40:28-31 (NASB) "DO YOU NOT KNOW? HAVE YOU NOT HEARD? THE EVERLASTING GOD, THE LORD, THE CREATOR OF THE ENDS OF THE EARTH DOES NOT BECOME WEARY OR TIRED. HIS UNDERSTANDING IS INSCRUTABLE. HE GIVES STRENGTH TO THE WEARY, AND TO HIM WHO LOCKSMITH HE INCREASES POWER. THOUGH YOUTHS GROW WEARY AND TIRED, AND VIGOROUS MEN STUMBLE BADLY, YET THOSE WHO WAIT UPON THE LORD WILL GAIN NEW STRENGTH; THEY MOUNT UP WITH WINGS LIKE EAGLES, THEY WILL RUN AND NOT GET TIRED, THEY WILL WALK AND NOT BECOME WEARY."**

2. Paul's Prayer (VS. 14-21)

This prayer focuses on knowing the characteristic as Christians and using those gifts, those traits in every aspect of our lives.

For our prayer to move a mountain our position must be subordinate to His will. It's about a heart posture of brokenness and bending to His will.

In verse 14-15, Paul emphasizes his posture (it must have been quite an ordeal for his Roman soldiers who were chained to him). However the position to "bow" (in the NKJV) is not necessarily what we have to do physically to get God's attention, it is a matter of the heart. When our heart is bowed in accordance to God's will, when we are subject to His word, when we say "God I want what you want"... then we see prayer move the heart of the King (Proverbs 21:1). For our prayer to move a mountain, our position must be subordinate to His will. It's about a heart posture of brokenness and bending to His will.

Paul prayed for four things in verses 16-19:

① **He prayed for strength.** He begged that their/our spirits would be strengthened. This is what allows us to live and act like Jesus, our "inner man". He prayed that the Holy Spirit would permeate our lives. It penetrates our souls and our lives absorb His truth like a sponge. The Holy Spirit can refresh and revitalize us from the inside; even when our bodies grow weak, our inner being can be strong.

② **He prayed for depth.** He prayed for Christians to be grounded, to be rooted in the love of Christ. He wants us to know that this love is not based on what we can do for God (not works based). This love is an agape love, a love grounded on a decision Jesus made on the cross. Agape love always involves sacrifice, unselfishness. It is a love that is fixed; it is not circumstantial.

So when we accept the depth of this love, we develop roots. This gives a visual picture of a mature, steady tree that will not be shaken when storms hit. When we as believers comprehend the depth of Jesus's love for us, it propels us into walking secure and confident towards our destiny- our appointed calling. Paul wants us to be more than saved; he wants Christ to dwell in our hearts. He uses the two Greek words, "kata" (down) and "oikos" (house), literally translated, "to settle down and feel at home." Paul wants Jesus to settle in to our lives, not be a guest. The picture is the owner of the house (Jesus) to come in and cleans it up and renovates-remodels.

③ **He prayed for comprehension.** Paul desired believers to experience the love of God, not just have knowledge of it. He wanted us to make it our own. He knew that when we experience the love of God truly, then we could in turn transfer it to others.

④ **He prayed for fullness.** Paul wanted us to be overflowing with the Holy Spirit. This is allowing God into the deepest recesses of your heart and mind; it is a quest to know Him more and be possessed by Him more completely. It means to follow His guiding, His promptings.
Then Paul closes with a doxology, literally a "word of glory" (Greek doxa, "glory + logos, "word").

> **EPHESIANS 3:20-21 (NLT) "NOW ALL GLORY TO GOD, WHO IS ABLE, THROUGH HIS MIGHTY POWER AT WORK WITHIN US, TO ACCOMPLISH INFINITELY MORE THAN WE MIGHT ASK OR THINK. 21 GLORY TO HIM IN THE CHURCH AND IN CHRIST JESUS THROUGH ALL GENERATIONS FOREVER AND EVER! AMEN."**

Look at His immeasurable power! That power lives in us as believers! The great saints of history did miracles because of that power. God has shared His great power with us to glorify Christ, to bring people to Him. What is keeping us from experiencing His richness, His fullness? Why are we as Christians at times so deficient? Why do have so many "power outages"?

Lessons Learned:

1. I have confident and complete access to God. (Hebrews 4:16; Hebrews 10: 19-23; Psalms 145:18)

2. God loves me. It is a decision love. I cannot earn it. (Romans 5:8; Psalm 86:15; John 3:16)

3. Nothing is impossible with God. (Matthew 7:11; Matthew 19:26; Jeremiah 32:17)

Group Questions:

1. We have equal access to salvation (vs. 6; 2:11,22). Why is this a big deal?
(Romans 6:23; Hebrews 10:19; Isaiah 55:6-7;James 5:16; Hebrews 4:15-16) Free gift of God is eternal life. Blood of Jesus; Jesus can sympathize because he was on earth, yet without sin.

2. The Mystery of reconciliation was Paul's anthem (Acts 9:15; 26:13-18). This unity between the Jews and the Gentiles meant prison for Paul. If you stand for the gospel it may cost you, what does the Bible have to say about this? Have you experienced difficulties telling someone about Jesus or even inviting him or her to church?
(Matthew 5:10-12; John 15:18; Luke 14:27; 1 Peter 3:14)
Blessed are those who are persecuted for righteousness sake, for theirs is the Kingdom of God. World hated Jesus first.

3. What does it mean to know the love of Christ (v 19)? How does that knowledge transform us? What does it look like in our day-to-day lives?
(1 John 4:9-12; John 17:26; John 15:12; Matthew 5:44; Galatians 6:2; Matthew 5:16) Bear one anothers burden, let your light shine, love one another as I have loved you.

4. What do these verses say about God's power toward believers:
(2 Timothy 1:7; 2 Corinthians 12:9; Colossians 1:28-29;
1 Corinthians 2:2-5; Ephesians 3:16; 2 Peter 1:2-4)
Love, dicipline, not timidy + fear
Power works in weakness
Holy Spirit

John Ortberg in his blog post Valuable Raggedness posted on December 6, 2013, he tells the story of his sister Barbie and her favorite doll when she was growing up, a doll named Pandy. "When Pandy, the doll, was young and perfect, Barbie loved her. She loved her with a love that was too strong for Pandy's own good. When Barbie went to bed at night, Pandy lay next to her. When Barbie had lunch, Pandy ate beside her at the table. When Barbie could get away with it, Pandy took a bath with her. Barbie's love for that doll, from Pandy's point of view, was nearly a fatal attraction.

By the time I knew Pandy she was not a particularly attractive doll. In fact, to tell the truth, she was a mess. She had lost a good deal of her hair, one of her arms was missing, and generally speaking, she'd had the stuffing knocked out of her. But for reasons that no one could ever quite figure out, in the way that kids sometimes do, my sister Barbie loved that little rag doll still. She loved her as strongly in the days of Pandy's raggedness as she ever had in her days of great beauty. Other dolls came and went; but Pandy was family. Love Barbie; love her rag doll. It was a package deal.

Once we took a vacation from our home in Rockford, Illinois, to Canada. We had returned almost all the way home when we realized at the Illinois border that Pandy had not come back with us. She had remained behind at the hotel in Canada. No other option was thinkable. My father turned the car around, and we drove from Illinois all the way back to Canada. We rushed into the hotel and checked with the desk clerk in the lobby, no Pandy. We ran back up to our room, still no Pandy. We ran downstairs and found the laundry room, Pandy was there, wrapped up in the sheets about to be washed to death."

John Ortberg then makes this observation: "The measure of my sister's love for that doll was that she would travel all the way to a distant country to save her. [Even though Pandy was more rag than doll, Barbie loved her with a love that made Pandy beautiful.]

My daughter Caroline has a blanket like that. My mom knitted her a pink blanket before she was born she slept with it, ate with it, did everything a human could do with a non-human thing. That blanket was disgusting even after countless washes. It smelled awful, lost it's pink color, even became yarn strings, but Caroline loved it! My mom made her a new one- she wanted the old one. She wouldn't travel- wouldn't sleep- wouldn't relax without that run down, decrepit, funky smelling, faded, more string-than material blanket. I am so glad Jesus loves me like that! He loves me flawed, broken, wounded and bent. But He desires me anyway. He dies for me anyway. The most wonderful aspect about Jesus is that He redeems my raggedness, but He also restores me. Actually He does better; He turns me in into a "New Creation". He loves me so much He does not leave me the way He found me. He creates out of a damaged, troubled rag doll; He fashions a priceless treasure.

God's love, agape, is a love beyond reason. It doesn't make sense. It's a love that is undeserved and sacrificial. It can never be earned. God's love for you is simply because He has chosen to do so. It is not rational. It is not explainable. It is just because it's God. We are broken people loved by an infinite, irrational, uncontainable loving God; because of His love we can reaching out to anyone from a different world, tear down walls, share our radical faith stories in the name of our Savior.

Notes

Shine

Chapter 4: Ephesians 4:1-16

God's Plan for Partnerships

God's **Plan** for ~ Partnerships ~

Paul moves from what God has done to what we get to do. He moves from life changing theology to mind stretching application. Ephesians is the perfect balance between acceptance and assignment, between doctrines and duties. Ephesians deals with the core of Christianity and the very practice of being a Christian. Paul is building the spiritual house, the Church— we begin works together, every component balances each other, every part of the body functions as a whole. He wanted to protect against future problems by admonishing the believers at the Ephesian church to mature, to grow up in their faith. But this message is not just for the Ephesians church; Paul is confronting us all to elevate our thinking, to change our perspective.

Paul is challenging us to use what we have been given. He urges to run, not walk. Paul desired the Christians in the church of Ephesus to make a difference in the world in the name of Jesus. He questions immaturity in a believer in this chapter- he tells us to grow up. He urges us to use our gifts and build the body of Christ to impact our community for Jesus.

Paul focused on Unity as believers, now in chapters 4-6 we will see how that can be achieved. God indicates that because He has given us a calling and equipped us for His purpose, we now must live up to that calling. Our mission is to glorify Jesus with our words and actions.

We should lift Jesus up with the words that we speak (Ephesians 4:29) and we model the love that He shows us with our actions toward others (John 15:12). Living like Jesus is our practical response to our new position as children of God.

Unity in the Body (vs. 1-16)

Paul Billheimer in his book **Love Covers** said, "The continuous and widespread fragmentation of the Church has been the scandal of the ages. It has been Satan's master strategy. The sin of disunity probably has caused more souls to be lost than all other sins combined."

St. Augustine said the two rules for Christian living are to love God and love your neighbors. Augustine considered the love of your neighbor as preparation for or even inseparable from your love for God. He viewed loving God is acted out by loving your neighbor. So think about this, how can you say you love Jesus and you can't even love your neighbor? I know. I completely get it. That is the hardest thing about being a Christian- applying the knowledge. Basically in a nutshell, our lives are viewed by people around us as living testimonies of God's grace to them. When we show them love, it is as if God is showing them love.

1. Let's get along (vs 1-3)

EPHESIANS 4:3 (NLT) "MAKE EVERY EFFORT TO KEEP YOURSELVES UNITED IN THE SPIRIT, BINDING YOURSELF TOGETHER WITH PEACE."

We get to partner with an Almighty Creator to reach an unsaved creation; He has called and qualified the broken and wounded to carry hope, to carry peace. We are bridge- builders, world- changers.

In verse two, Paul says, "walk worthy in your calling"; that is not communicated like physical walking, but it is actually how we conduct ourselves. The conduct of our lives should exemplify what God has called us to do. What is our calling? I am so glad you asked. We are called to: Glorify God (Ephesians 1:3-14).

Glorifying God will lead us to be a part of a body of Christ that does good works, that tells others about Him, that praises Him and loves each other.

In verse three, Paul places an emphasis on the topic of unity; unity is derived in believers when knowledge of our eternal purpose is our complete focus. Unifying love for the body of Christ, to do good for the family of God has two aims: it is a witness to the world, and it is an acclamation of the glory of God.

Paul lists relational characteristics we must pursue and practice to manifest the unity and glorify God. All of these elements are freely given to us by the grace of God. They are the fruit of our relationship with Him. **Remember fruit is a product-if you want more fruit you will plant more seeds.** If you desire more spiritual fruit, you grow in your relationship with Jesus-Prayer, Bible reading, Church attendance, etc.

A. Our lives should be marked by humility. Humility is not thinking less of you; it is thinking more of God. Humility is realizing that God has endowed us with special, unique abilities to use for His glory, and all good things come from Him.

B. Our lives should be marked by gentleness. This is the concept of strength under control. The visual picture of a powerful horse under the bridle and it is completely obedient to the tug on the reins from the master. It is power under control. Handling people with kindness. Visualize their hurts behind the problems.

We are not independent of each other we are interdependent on each other and God.

C. Our lives should be marked by patience. Remembering God's long-suffering kindness toward us while we were sinners prompts patience. It is withholding judgment, the ability to endure discomfort without striking back. It also implies commitment.

2. Prove you get along (vs 4-6)

This section is connected by the word "One". We are not independent of each other- we are interdependent on each other and God. This section also shines a light on the great assets we have as members of God's family.

A. One Body. Every person, at salvation, belongs to the body of Christ. In addition, but you also need to belong to another body, a body of believers, the local church where you can exercise your gifts and talents. The word "body" is used here more times than any other book of the Bible- to show the importance of realizing the oneness of the Church. You cannot harm one part of the body without affecting another part.

B. One Spirit. The Holy Spirit indwells us at the moment of salvation giving us the power to thrive like Christ. We literally become what the Bible calls the "temple of God" (1 Corinthians 6:19-20). The same spirit that lives inside you inhabits me, and within every believer. If we are saved- if we have accepted Jesus Christ as the only way to Heaven, as a payment for our sins the Holy Spirit dwells inside us and unites us as one.

C. One Hope. The hope of Heaven, we don't live, as Earth is our final destiny. The word "hope" refers to a "deep settled confidence based on the clear word of God."

D. One Lord. Jesus died, buried, and rose from the grave to give us life. Jesus is the head and gives direction and wisdom (Romans 10:12).

E. One Faith. The faith that Jesus deposited in His early church (Jude 3). The doctrinal truths of the Bible unite believers. Our truth is anchored in the Word of God.

The fact that we are unified does not distract from the reality that God made us unique.

F.One Baptism. Paul spoke here of water baptism which is an outward picture, public declaration of God's work common in every believer. Baptism is a means of identification. It is an outward symbol of what happened inwardly.

G. One God and Father. This is God the Father (did you notice 7 things- the number of perfection?). This placement "above all" strategically places God as the author, as sovereign. He is "through all" which describes His omnipresence; God is everywhere in all places at all times. He is "in you all" emphasizes the indwelling of the Holy Spirit, the part of God that lives inside us at the moment of salvation. One Father created one family. One Son gave us one faith, one hope, and one baptism. One Spirit has created one body.

3. Possessions to help you get along (vs 7-11)

The fact that we are unified, does not distract from the reality that God made us unique. God has given every believer at least one spiritual gift (1 Corinthians 12:1-12) and this gift is to be used with grace to reach a common goal, to glorify God and serve each other. The Bible pictures the church as a body; each part has a special job. Every person at birth was allocated certain talents and natural abilities. When a person accepts Jesus as their Savior, as the only way to Heaven they receive spiritual gifts from Christ. God has given us unique gifts to be used in the church. There are three places these gifts are listed: 1 Corinthians 12, Romans 12, and Ephesians 4. In Ephesians 4 we are looking at the gifts that unify the church.

A. Apostles (vs. 11a) The apostolic gift refers to those who were sent with authority. It also points to the founders of the church. Today we use the term to indicate those who lead a number of churches.

B. Prophets (vs. 11) This gift is used for one speaks for God, proclaims His word with divine anointing so listeners who understand this is truly the word of the Lord. This is not the same as an Old Testament prophet, which existed before the Bible was completed.

C. Evangelists (vs. 11) This gift refers to those who share and explain the Good News to unbelievers.

D. Pastors (vs. 11) This gift is attributed to the shepherds of God's people. They assume the care of God's people.

E. Teachers (vs. 11) The gift of teaching is seen on people who instruct and expound the scriptures to others for accuracy.

4. Purpose of getting along (vs 12-16)

Three things according to these verses define the end goal of spiritual maturity; like Jesus, stable (consistent), truth working cohesively with love.

Lessons Learned:

1. God calls me to be on a team for one purpose, to glorify Him.
(John 17:4; Isaiah 43:1-7; 1 Peter 4:11)

2. Unity does not mean the same. I am uniquely created.
(Psalm 139:13-18; Matthew 10:30; Jeremiah 1:4-5)

3. For God's Kingdom to expand every Christian must do their part. I have been redeemed at a high price. I get to partner with Him to reach my world.
(Philippians 2:13; Ephesians 2:8-10)

Group Questions:

1. What does "walking worthy" mean? How does it look on a daily basis in our life?
(Colossians 1:9-14; 1 John 2:6; 1 Thessalonians 2:12; Philippians 1:27)

2. What is the role of Christian Community in our spiritual growth? (Vs. 11-13) What does this process reveal about the necessity of Christian community for our growth?
(John 15:12; Galatians 5:13; Hebrews 10:24-25; Romans 15:14; Galatians 6:2)

3. Paul invites us to experience Christ deeper through significant involvement in the lives of other believers. What in our life can produce resistance to embracing other believers, thereby missing out on Christ's provision for our spiritual growth? How about this… how can embracing others produce spiritual fruit? (Proverbs 27:17; John 13:34-35; 1 Corinthians 12:24-26; John17:20-21)

4. What does it mean to partner with God to reach the world? (Deuteronomy 10:12-13; Matthew 5:14-16; Colossians 3:23-24)

Think again about unity… I have a difficult time riding in a car with my family for a long road trip, but I must admit I value peace and harmony. Cohesiveness, agreement, cooperation these words are synonyms of unity. In the best of situations unity is difficult to maintain.

A horse-pulling contest in Canada illustrates the effect of synergism especially well. The people put weights on a flat bed wagon, and a single horse pulled it a measured distance. They added 1,000 pounds at a time, until the horse could no longer pull it. The winner pulled 9,000 lbs., and the runner-up pulled 8,000 lbs. Out of curiosity, someone suggested putting those two horses together. When they hitched both horses to the wagon, they pulled 31,000 lbs. Working together the horses pulled more than three times the weight the best of them could pull alone. And so it is with humans. When we work together, we can accomplish much more than we can separately.

In the animated movie Ice Age, when saber-tooth tigers attack a tribe of nomads, a mother and her baby attempt to outrun the man-eating beasts but are cornered at a raging waterfall. The little boy is discover- red by a wooly mammoth named Manfred, a sloth name Sid, and a saber-tooth tiger named Diego. These three unlikely companions unite on a common mission to return the baby to his father.

As the trio treks through a mountainous terrain of ice and snow carrying the baby, at one point the mammoth, sloth, and tiger realize they're on an erupting volcano. The heat of the lava melts the glacier bridges atop the ice fields, separating Diego from the others. Isolated on a quickly melting island of ice, Diego jumps to reach the others, but falls short. Dangling from the edge of the ice field, his grip falters, and he falls. Manfred, unwilling to let Diego perish, leaps into a chasm after him and tosses the tiger upwards to safety. Diego, realizing the danger involved in the rescue, is moved by Manfred's compassion, courage, and sacrifice.

"Why did you do that?" he asks. "You could have died trying to save me."

Humbly, the mammoth responds, "That's what you do when you're part of a herd. You look after each other." Amazed at the convergence of circumstances that has brought these three together, Sid muses aloud.

Working together, building each other up, recognizing value in others, and keeping the focus on the important are keys to a unified, healthy, growing church that is concentrated on reaching others for Jesus.

Notes

Shine

Chapter 5: Ephesians 5:1-20

God's Pattern for our Performance

God's **Pattern** for our ~ Performance ~

We do not have to live in a confusing fog of what is right and wrong as a believer. God has given us a manual, a guidebook. Paul tells us to mimic Him, to imitate Him. Every work Jesus performed flowed from who He was- His love for people, His compassion. We can't be like Christ by just solely replicating His actions; we have to consider His motives and attitudes. So when we think of imitating Him we must first think about it coming from our core- our internal motives, our desires should be to carry out His will, to glorify Him.

A lot of people have heroes and most loved children want to mimic their parent. As a child I wanted to be near my dad, even being the only girl in the family I still would join in with my brothers and uncles when my dad took them hunting or fishing (even though I hated the smell of the fish and couldn't bait the hook myself). My uncles would get a kick out of me following along behind him in my pigtails trying to walk in his footsteps and stride just like him. I would try to cast my rod exactly as he would, I would use the same lure as he did (having no idea what I was doing). I just wanted to be like my dad and be with him.

The same principle applies with our relationship with Jesus. When he loves us we naturally want to be around Him and be like Him.

"To many Christians Christ is little more than an idea, or at best an ideal; He is not a fact. Millions of professed believers talk as if He were real and act as if He were not. And always, our actual position is to be discovered by the way we act, not by the way we talk."

AW. Tozer

1. Walk in love (vs 1-7)

The only thing that can make us want to break our natural tendency, the trend to place ourselves first, is the recognition of the depth of God's love. Look at what Paul says to emulate, His love, which is probably the most difficult and practical precept. Love encompasses large and small situations. Love never takes a break and is never finished. Love is a sacrifice. When the Bible says, "love your enemies" do you think that there is a loophole? And weren't we once the enemies? I have found in my time here on this dust-filled planet that enemies have actually driven me into my Father's arms; they have made me yearn for His embrace. So I guess we love our enemies not only because Jesus loves them, but also because He loved us, and because it draws us nearer to Him.

Paul's point is that we are a new creation in Christ and we demonstrate this new life by relying on the power of the Holy Spirit, and He enables us to control our behavior through the lenses of love. We can love others because He loved us. The love we have for others is the modeled by Jesus. He emptied Himself; He humbled Himself, and He offered Himself. When Paul goes into detail in verse 2 about the offering and sacrifice to God as a "fragrant aroma" he is thinking of two scenarios: one, the aroma of the sacrifice, the bloody, irony smell that symbolized sin was paid in complete; and he also imagined in 2 Corinthians 2:14-16, Christ marching in Triumph where generals, state officials, priests swinging incense depicting the sweet smell of joy and triumph.

Paul understood that the city of Ephesus was desperately wicked and he knew of the temptations the Christians faced at that time and we also face at this time. He warned them against immorality, the Greek word is actually "porneia" and it is referring to any sexual relationship outside of marriage. "Greed" literally means the desire to have more whether it is directed at money or anything else.

These are both derived from uncontrolled appetites. Paul goes on to list speaking patterns. Paul tells us to "watch your mouth"! He actually lists "foolish talk" which is translated from the Greek "morologia", literally the talk of fools. Paul goes on to say in verses 5-6 that if someone consistently practices these vices they are in opposition to the commands of Jesus, and no one can live comfortably without a clear conscience. One version of scripture warns us to steer away from people dabbling continuously in sin. Truly the difference is not killing ourselves by saying "no" to sin, but saying "yes" to Jesus. Pulling closer to Him means we are pushing away from sin. Pursuing the heart of God means the less time we have to stalk the desires of our selfishness.

Pursuing the heart of God means the less time we have to stalk the desires of our selfishness.

2. Walk in Light (vs 8-14)

Remember why we do this... why we have a standard of holiness...because we aren't like them. Really we aren't! We are children of the light; which means the darkness, death from sin, is now removed by the sacrificial blood of Jesus and replaced by the light of Jesus Christ. In John 1:5 the Bibles says, "The light shines in the darkness and the darkness has not overcome it." The Greek word is actually "katalabano"- "comprehend" The darkness doesn't even understand the light inside of us, the darkness that is clawing to capture your child can't even comprehend the light of a praying mama. God's character is light and since He dwells in us (remember at the moment of salvation the Holy Spirit part of the Trinity); He generates the products of God's character inside of us. When we are light we affect a dark world. Light exposes darkness and it erases darkness. Light can not only reveal- it will also transform!

3. Walk in Wisdom (vs 15-20)

Paul reminds us again that walking is simply putting a string of steps together and repeating. That's what the Christian life is... focus! Be careful! Stay steady! Walk! Actually the first few words of verse 15 tell us to be careful and be aware, but also don't miss out on what we have in Christ! Know your enemy but more importantly know who is on your side! Verse 15 is encouraging us to be wise, which in practical terms is someone who can take God's Word and apply it to their life. Wisdom is the ability to use the Bible as a manuscript for living, making the most of every opportunity.

In verse 18, Paul warns the believer not to get drunk. Paul doesn't want the Christian to be mastered, to be controlled by someone other than God. However, Paul does encourage us to continually be filled with the Spirit. The Holy Spirit lives in us at salvation but the filling is the maturing process He does on a daily basis. The word "filled" carries the meaning "to be full to the top; lacking nothing; nothing short of complete." If there is any room for anything else we need to check ourselves. I have heard someone say that the Holy Spirit doesn't want to just be a resident; He wants to be president of our lives.

D.L. Moody said, "God commands us to be filled with the Spirit, and if we are not filled it is because we are living beneath our privileges."

People that are under the influence of the Holy Spirit will want to outwardly express their relationship. When the Holy Spirit controls us, it spills out. Worship is an outpouring of our gratefulness to the Lord. I love how in Psalm 100 the Psalmist David tells us to make a "joyful noise" to the Lord; we don't have to have perfect pitch, it is about the heart. Worship sends the enemy running. When we sing the praises of

God the more the evil one hears His lies defeated. Thanksgiving is another by-product of a spirit-filled heart. When we are filled with the spirit- consistently walking with Him, listening to Him, reading His word, it flows outwards. When we give thanks, we see God's goodness and grace amidst our fallen world. We choose to be grateful.

Lessons Learned:

1. Spirit-filled believers are the light of the world, and the world desperately needs to see the light!
(Matthew 5:13-16; 1 Peter 2:9; Acts 13:17; John 8:12)

2. The filling of the Holy Spirit changes my behavior. It is a constant awareness of His presence and power in any situation.
(Romans 8:26; Galatians 5:22-23; John 14:16-17; John 16:7-11,13)

3. Genuine worship results from a heart that is overwhelmed by the majesty and presence of our great God.
(Matthew 12:34; Hebrews 13:15; Psalm 103:1-5)

Group Questions:

1. Compare a life of darkness with a life composed of light. (1 John 2:9-11; 1 Peter 4:3-5; Philippians 2:14-16; Romans 12:2)

2. Read Ephesians verses 8-20. What does living in the light look like? Practically. Walking is a great analogy; remember it's a conglomeration of steps, one step at a time. How can we encourage each other to "walk in the light"?

3. Our words have the power of life or death. This chapter dives into words of worship and "moronic", filthy words, and empty words. We see extremes and realize that what you say flows from what is in your heart (Luke 6:45). How can we make our words breathe life?
(James 1:19; Acts 20:32; Psalm 141:3; Proverbs 12:18; Matthew 15:18)

4. We studied a little about worship and we all know that sometimes in difficulties it is tough to praise God. Read Acts 16:16-25, 26-40… describe this scene and tell me what happens when we decide to worship through desperate situations.
(Job 1:20-22; Habakkuk 3:17-19; Hebrews 13:8; Psalm 34:18; Psalm 9:9)

Sacrificial love is totally and completely selfless. It is unconditional. It is always giving. It is actually a suffering love. It is a love that involves bearing others weaknesses and failings. God loved us so much that He sacrificed His only Son to die a horrific death. He sacrificed His Son; we, of course, probably won't have to do that. But to show Jesus to our neighbors we may be called to love the unlovely, to be kind to the unkind, and to be generous to the miserly. It is not just a Valentine's Day thing-it is an all year, every day, and all person thing. When we know God, we know love. To give love when it cost something, even when it hurts, that is giving God. Loving like Jesus is to start from the cross and end at the cross.

There are endless examples of courage buried in the ruins of the Holocaust, but Irena Sendler's story stands out. When the Nazis invaded her native Poland and rounded up all the Jews into a walled in ghetto, Sendler knew what was going to happen. She was a social worker and worked to get credentials as a nurse so she could sneak food and medicine into the ghetto. What she snuck out was even more phenomenal: It's estimated that Sendler and her group helped get approximately 2,500 children out of the ghetto—sedated and placed in the bottom of toolboxes or lying in burlap sacks at the bottom of her truck—and sent them through a network of likeminded comrades to Christian orphanages, where they were given new identities. She kept their real names in a jar buried in her backyard. Eventually, the Nazis, caught Sendler, imprisoned and tortured her, breaking both of her legs. When the war ended she devoted herself to reuniting children with their families. True love sacrifices.

Notes

Shine

Chapter 6: Ephesians 5:21-6:9

God's Pattern for Propinquity

God's **Pattern** for ~ Propinquity ~

Propinquity is how people can get along together living in close proximity to each other. The Bible instructs us on the subject of relationships that are the closest to us. How do you get along with your family? I have found the closer in vicinity someone is and the closer in relationship someone is with me, the easier it is to hurt them. What I mean is the significance of the relationship makes me feel so safe that I allow myself to be cruel or at the time (I may call it "real" or even "truthful"). There are actually studies based on this fact; the idea that we hurt the ones we love. Scripture is showing us how we can overcome this natural desire for reciprocity. This practical concept is the heartbeat of realistic theology, placing your needs secondary to the needs of others. I believe it is very appropriate that in the previous chapter we discussed sacrificial love because in the relationships closest to us that's when we view its strategic application. Sometimes it's easier to be kind to a stranger than your kid when he is "getting on that last nerve"; or it's less of a burden to go out of our way for someone at the office than to put a little more effort or be helpful to our spouse. Sacrificial, agape love is unconditional, giving love. It devotes total commitment to seek your highest best no matter how anyone may respond. Agape love is a verb, not a noun. It is a decision and an action.

"A good marriage is a contest of generosity." Diane Sawyer www.azquotes.com/quote/520643

1. Husbands/Wives (vs 21-33)

Marriage is a divine institution. It is probably the most intricate, complex relationship on the earth. Marriage is not a power struggle where the strongest or most domineering wins. Marriage is not an economic partnership that is characterized by management. Marriage is not a fairy tale where one is put on a pedestal, or a gold throne in the castle. Marriage is a one-flesh relationship; it's a level of physical, emotional, financial, social, and spiritual intimacy that represents Jesus' love for the church.

Just a reminder of what we looked at in verses 18-21… we looked at maturity spiritual holiness…growing up to be like Jesus. The key to living like Jesus is unselfishness, which comes through maturity. The effect of that maturity is mutual submission. Mutual submission is defined as serving someone else, not ourselves. The word "submit" does have strong connotations, and can be daunting. I have heard it called the Text of Terror, seriously. Let's look where else it is used in the Bible. Jesus voluntarily submitted to Mary and Joseph as a child in Luke 2:51. It is used when King David appointed his young son Solomon as king and the mighty men pledged their allegiance to him in 1 Chronicles 29:24. Jesus submitted to the will of the Father on the cross. I, honestly, love this idea of voluntarily choosing to give my husband my allegiance and honor. It leaves the ball in may court, so to speak. I am choosing that I have the power to gift my husband the privilege of leading. Submission was used 16 times in the Old Testament; in reference to God (remember Jesus submitted to the Father) it generally had strong military connotations. Based on that fact it makes sense that God created women to be warriors! This is what God is asking wives to do to come along side their husbands and help him to magnify the Lord. He called us a "Help-mate" in Genesis 2:18. It is a yielding, we are equal in creation, but have different roles.

The wife's abilities have nothing to do with the mindset of submission. Submission is a God given calling, as a wife to honor and affirm her husband's leadership; submission is mutually beneficial; it is an attitude that pours from our heart. But do not let me mislead you; we will struggle with this because it is contrary to our nature. I know I am not very good at saying "No" to myself. Remember a submissive wife isn't a doormat, not a mute, not a robot. She sees value in herself and her husband. But she is fiercely committed with a quiet confidence in her husband, she encourages him, she accepts his Godly leadership in the home, and she is his biggest cheerleader. Submission is far more easily identified by its absence than its presence. Remember a two-headed animal in the natural world doesn't live very long. Let me give you some easy, common "what it can look like" handles: respecting his lead, being receptive, and acting responsive to input, encouraging with actions and attitudes.

Love is an internal decision; your attitude and actions will lead to love. Love stimulates love.

In verse 25, we identify the directions given to the husband. The husband gets the privilege of loving his wife. But this isn't just any kind of love; this is an unconditional, sacrificial, giving love. A love that doesn't have to be reciprocated and it's committed to the highest good. Paul points out the example of Jesus' love for us. He was nailed to the cross taking our sin, the sin of all mankind when He had no sin. Jesus died an excruciating death, separated from His Father, all for love. Steven Cole wrote, "A husband may say, 'I'd die for my wife if it ever came down to it. I'd fight to the death in order to protect her.' That's tremendous, and I hope you would! But here's the real question: Are you crucifying self on a daily basis on behalf of your wife?" The Bible tells the husband to love his wife, that's the priority. When the atmosphere of love is set, all else flows outward. Love is an internal decision; when you decide to love whether or not it is reciprocated, your attitude and actions will lead to love.

Paul also used the word "sanctify" in one version, which simply means "set apart". A husband sets his wife above all others. He will seek to protect her holiness and purity. He will choose to love her and set her apart so that she will develop into the woman God has planned. (Vs. 26-27)

The key to both submitting and unconditional love is realizing that the strength doesn't come from us, it is from the Holy Spirit that dwells inside of us; He enables us to do things that are counterintuitive, countercultural. It allows us to leave the comfortable place of our parents and "cleave" to our spouses. The word "cleave" is the Greek word for glue, it called cement sometimes. The relationship is sealed! Let me fill you in on the culture of that period. Ephesus was awful. The people were putting their spouses away; one author said, "Wives were practical, not precious." When Paul said to love your wife as Christ loved the church, and wives weren't under strict law, they were loved! It went contrary to their upbringing. The shocker for Ephesians husbands was not that were the "heads", but that they were to love, even yield to their wives because of their deep respect for Jesus.

Jesus and his love for His bride, the Church, model all of this. Jesus sacrificed for the church, He died for us and He is faithful to us.

2. Parent/Child (vs 6:1-4)

It actually is a wonderful thing that we see God address children in these verses; the Roman Empire was exceptionally callous in their view of children, just like women. Children were not wanted. Babies were abandoned due to economic reasons, birth defects, illegitimacy, evil omens, or gender. Children with birth defects were considered exceptionally challenging to provide financially and physically. When an Emperor died and a baby was born around that time parents would expose or abandon their newborns to the elements. These babies that were found could often have become slaves. But God elevated children by addressing them directly! God instructed kids to obey their parents because it is right. The Bible also commands us to honor our parents. Honor is more than obedience; it involves respect and placing importance on that person. Honor isn't about "honorability"; it's what we are called to do. As adult children, honor is apparent in our kindness and our grace. It is visible through esteem. Small acts can show honor even for adult kids of dysfunctional families as Christ followers; we are compelled to show honor. We can give their perspective value; acknowledge their advice. For kids under our roof though while we are paying the bills—obedience is not just an action it is also an attitude that is demonstrated by honor. Sullen, slow, reluctant obedience is not obedience; it is actually resentment and bitterness, which will build up and eat away inside. As we cultivate obedience in our children we are encouraging a lifetime of obedience to God, which leads to a foundation of respect for authority. The blessing of obedience is a promise of "it will be well" and a "long life". This is a principle not a quantity, but quality of life. Obedience is a foundational principle that our children can apply to their lives in spiritual matters as well and see God perform miracles.

In verse 4, fathers (parents) have an admonition to not provoke children to anger (or resentment). Parents must be responsible to train and correct their children, but overly harsh punishments, being overly strict; being inconsistent, these are a few things that lead to exasperation, anger or discouragement (Colossians 3:21). The word picture is to cause your child's soul to shrivel into small hard, angry shells. Remember when you are drained and hard you will be hard and drain! Anger is the eroding emotion; it eats all the tender feelings. The remedy is to remember how Jesus teaches us. As parents we need to bring them up (the word used is like "nourishment" the implication of care behind the discipline is deep love and concern). We are to train our children (2 Timothy 3:16 this involves giving our children the abilities and character necessary to live a life pleasing to God); and we are to instruct our children, the force of this word actually has the concept of warning behind it. Discipline and instruction mentioned in verse 4 involves setting boundaries and consequences. Let me quickly clarify, this is also loving your child! When you love your child you discipline them, when you discipline and instruct you are acting like God. The Greek word for instruction is "nouthesia", which means to help a person by placing into their minds things that will benefit them. You are not just setting rules for your children; you are putting them in a position of blessing.

You are not just setting rules for your children; you are putting them in a position of blessing.

3. Employer/Employee (vs 5-9)

Paul addresses slavery in this section; there were an estimated 60,000 slaves in Ephesus during this Roman era (www.ephesus.us/ephesus/slavery_in_ephesus.htm).

It has been calculated that 60 million slaves made up the Roman Empire, literally one third of the empire. Paul was preaching to the slaves whether freed or not in his church, the church at Ephesus. Paul does not advocate slavery in this passage; He is merely addressing this large group of people who make up a significant part of the Christian population. He reminded them that their duty is only temporary; Heaven is our home, and God will leave no wrong unaddressed. Paul admonishes them to be Christ like in their positions. The great message of Jesus to everyone is that where God has placed us we get to live out the Christian life. But we see his stance on slavery reiterated by the writing of the book of Philemon where Paul sent Onesimus, a slave, to Philemon and told him to treat him like a brother.

To apply this passage to our lives we view and apply the principles to our relationship as employees and employers. There should be no separation between our "church life" and our "work life".

The first section verse tells us as employees to "be obedient", basically to do our jobs. We are challenged to do our best, not to please our bosses (remember Paul was writing to slaves) but to please God. An Employer should treat their employee with respect (again this was revolutionary when Paul was writing this) and be fair and reasonable with expectations. God rewards.

Lessons Learned:

1. God has ordained authority. Proper authority honors God and brings peace.
(Romans 13:1-2; Hebrews 13:17; Daniel 4:17)

2. Focus on blessings and benefits not rules and regulations of relationships. Attitudes are the soil that actions grow from.
(1 Corinthians 15:33; Proverbs 4:23; Psalm 119:31)

3. My relationship with Christ transforms my work performance.
(2 Corinthians 5:17; Ezekiel 36:26; Philippians 2:13)

Group Questions:

1. Submission is not the same as obedience. Both involve responses to authority, however the difference is obedience is simply an external reaction whereas submission is yielding; it involves willingness, a choice of compliance. Practically speaking, what does "submit" look like in a daily basis for us as 20th century believers?
(Proverbs 31:25, 26, 31; 12:4; Galatians 2:20; Philippians 2:4)

2. What does it look like for a husband to love his wife as Christ loved the Church and gave Himself up for her?
(1 John 4:19-21; 1 Peter 2:21-23; Galatians 5:13)

3. If we desire our children to love and follow God, what steps must we take to see this become a reality?
(John 13:35; Deuteronomy 6:4-9; Proverbs 22:6; James 5:16; Hebrews 12:9-11)

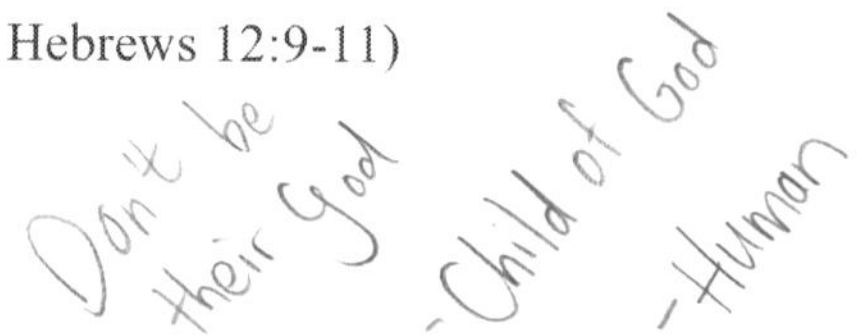

4. How do you view work? How does God view work?
(Colossians 3:22- 4:1; Psalm 121:4; Proverbs 14:23; Ecclesiastes 9:10)

Serving each other in close relationships is where the "rubber meets the road". It can be the most trying part of the day, to go home and be "like Jesus" (yes, I admitted it). Relationships are risky and are tough. But God called us to develop those relationships, He wants us to pour into our home life and live our Christianity so others may see His goodness and mercy. God has called us out of our broken and bruised lives to partner with Him and introduce healing and hope into our homes.

"Our families are small communities, and within them we experience a 'magnitude' of opportunities for service. We're accustomed to thinking of Christian service in terms that are nobler, more dramatic, more like Mother Teresa in the slums of Calcutta or Florence Nightingale on the battlefields of the Crimean war."

"But even for women like Mother Teresa and Florence Nightingale, service boils down to simple assistance in 'trifling, external things.' This means things as matching socks, packing lunches, or wiping kitchen tables. 'Be faithful in little things,' Mother Teresa advises, 'for in them our strength lies."

"Self-righteous, self-centered service demands visible external rewards, but the sort of service that Jesus modeled doesn't concern itself with results. Instead, it's content even with obscurity."

"Jeremy Taylor's 'Rule and Exercises of Holy Living,' written in the seventeenth century, says that we should 'love to be concealed, and little esteemed; be content to lack praise, never be troubled when thou art slighted or undervalued.' We need to remind ourselves that our value springs from God's love. We find our truest identities in the midst of His unmerited grace."
(Ellyn Sanna wrote in A Gentle Spirit)

Notes

Shine

Chapter 7: Ephesians 6:10-24

God's Principles for Power

Our **Principles** ~ for Power~

Sooner or later we will be compelled to jump out of our comfort zone and into the fire to go to battle. Maybe you are in a war right now, you may be shooting arrows or firing shots or feel like you're being shot at all day every day. Put your waterproof mascara on because we are going to war! Get your stilettos polished… or maybe you should pull out your flats. You probably are saying, "No kidding, my life appears to be one conflict after another."

Paul ends this enlightening book of Ephesians with a practical explanation and a gift to us. A warning. We are going into battle, not against our husbands, not our neighbors, not our exes, not our bosses, but against the devil. Did anyone have those plastic knight kits? My brothers and I had them and would go to "war" quite often. They didn't do much damage to me thankfully, and I didn't do any damage to my brothers, not because I wasn't trying. With our armor that God provides we can not only survive in a hostile environment, but also we can thriveuntil Jesus returns.

"We cannot stand the wiles of the devil by our wits. The devil only comes along the lines that God understands, not along the lines we understand, and the only way we can be prepared for him is to do what God tells us, stand complete in His armor, indwelt by His Spirit, in complete obedience to Him."
- Oswald Chambers

Put your waterproof mascara on because we are going to war!

1. Adversary (vs 10-12)

EPHESIANS 6:10 (NLT) "A FINAL WORD: BE STRONG IN THE LORD AND IN HIS MIGHTY POWER."

This verse tells us the same God who is going to throw Satan into the pit, the same God who sits on the throne and that everyone will bow down to at the end, can strengthen us. That same God lives inside of believers, He is the one who gives us strength. We need strength for two reasons: To do good and to stop doing bad. It seems simple and it actually boils down to that simple statement. God lives in us and gives us strength to do good and not do bad.

The first rule of engagement is to understand your enemy. As Christians must realize that we have an enemy who constantly thinks about us and dreams up ways in which to ensnare us. He constantly temps us to sin and do some act that will cause us to stumble in our faith and witness, and thus keep us from being used of God. Satan also tries to keep every unsaved person from understanding the gospel message and placing their faith and trust in Jesus Christ as their Lord and Savior. More than anything the Devil would like to take as many people on this earth to hell with him, as many as he can. His main objective is to keep people from the truth and hold them in spiritual bondage. Satan desires us blind to the victory that has already been won, blinded to the good news of the gospel, the freedom of Jesus.

2. Arms (vs 13-17)

We are called into active duty not to be just bystanders. We are fighting a spiritual war and we use spiritual weapons. God has equipped us to do battle, not just do battle but to have a victory! These are not passive weapons every one of these armaments come with a directive. It is up to us daily to be prepared... to put on... Remember it tells, "be strong". The Bible tells us to "resist the devil and he will flee". However to do spiritual battle, you must have spiritual weapons. We must have supernatural power that can only come from the Holy Spirit. This is not just "Let go and let God" this is an admonishment to get in there and do battle, to rely on His might, but also fight! As Christians we are totally inadequate without Christ, but with Him we have all the strength and tools necessary to defeat Satan and his forces.

A. Belt of Truth - The belt of a soldier is where he would carry his weapons, but it would also protect his abdomen and lower back. A soldier would tuck his robe or tunic in the belt to move quickly. This type of belt was fastened by the wearer, implying you can only do this yourself. No one can make this decision for you. Truth is in Jesus; the source is Jesus. Truth embodies Jesus Christ it is who He is and what He has accomplished (Isaiah 59:14-17). In order to place the belt of truth on our hips we make the decision to give Christ the ultimate authority over our lives. The belt is the foundational piece of weaponry and represents our belief and trusts in Jesus as our source of hope and provides stability. "Girding the loins" was a sign of readiness, preparation place of steadiness.

B. Breastplate of Righteousness - The breastplate covered the soldier from neck to waist, front to back. It protected the warrior's heart and vital organs. In the Hebrews' belief, the heart represented the mind, the emotions, the will, all the areas that Satan tries to attack us. When we guard our heart, putting on the righteousness of God; we are telling the devil our righteousness is Jesus righteousness. The Bible calls this "Imputed Righteousness". Plainly put, when we believe that Jesus' blood pays for all our sins, His righteousness, His perfection covers us. Satan will always attempt to accuse us, "you aren't good enough", "you did this" and on and on but we point to the righteousness of Jesus, the sinlessness of the Savior. However, there is another part to this, we are not saved by good works, but we are saved to do good works. Faith that is genuine, real, living, growing, produces righteousness. Righteousness is a result of my surrender to Him. The deeds flow from surrender.

C. Sandals of Peace - Roman soldiers wore sandals with thick cleats on the bottom to grip and dig in during battle. This peace stiletto keeps us focused, pointed in the right direction. When we prepare with peace, when our foundation is formed with the calm assurance that passes all understanding we are confident in proclaiming the good news of peace! As Christ followers, we must have a solid grasp, a sure footing, of the good news of the gospel so we can daily live in victory and experience that serene staidness ourselves. That confident knowledge of the good news of the gospel, that firm understanding of who He is and who I am because of Him enables me to stand firm in battle.

D. Shield of Faith - The Romans' shield was made out of leather, large enough to cover one man. The Romans would stand shoulder-to-shoulder forming a wall of protection against the flaming arrows. Before battle they would drench their shields with water to extinguish the fiery arrows. Faith is defined as "firm belief", a trust. A deep-rooted confidence in God will protect us. I love the picture of warriors lined up together, moving together using their faith as defense and offense. We are not alone! I think it is enlightening that God associated a shield with faith; a shield guards, defends, and deflects. Our faith through times of trouble will protect us when the devil shoots his fiery darts of uncertainty, our steadfast belief in God's love and goodness holds us true. Faith offers complete protection and makes advance possible. Faith knows where to turn when doubts and fears arise. Faith takes the blows that were meant for us; our shield can take the brunt. Our confidence in God and His Word is of no use unless it is well handled. One way is handle your shield by quoting verses when he shoots arrows of doubts at you. Another way we take up our shield of faith is by obeying His Word. My obedience becomes a shield in the face of the devil's deceit. We win by believing God.

My obedience becomes a shield in the face of the devil's deceit.

E. Helmet of Salvation - A Roman soldier who lost his helmet was in danger at the least of severe head wounds. This would render him ineffective and/or incapacitated. It could also kill him. The Roman soldier's helmet was intended to defend against a broadsword. Satan's broadsword has two sides to it: discouragement and doubt. Satan wants to knock you in the head with discouragement and doubt. The helmet of salvation protects our mind, our hope. This helmet of salvation speaks to the hope of heaven, the confidence in a complete total salvation from past, present, and future sin. Jesus paid it all! Again this is not reiterating the moment of trust in Jesus as Savior, the actual moment of salvation. Paul is referring to the times when believers are discouraged and encourages us to have that confidence in our eternal security that we already possess. It is the assurance that God will triumph. Hope paints the future in bright colors when we are discouraged or apprehensive. Hope speaks joy in our hour of sorrow or trial.

F. Sword of the Spirit - The Roman sword, known as the gladius, was a lethal weapon. It was acknowledged as "the sword that conquered the world". It was sharpened on both sides enabling it to pierce armor. This is our offensive weapon of choice the Holy, inspired Word of God. When we read the Bible God brings passages and verses to our path that meet our needs and counteract the conditions of our life. We stab the devil with the scripture, visually speaking.

Prayer is for wartime, not for domestic convenience. We don't use it like we are calling our concierge for room service.

Christians possess the sword of the spirit, which is the Word of God. We just need to pick it up and use it. The Bible is that sword. Not because we own one, but because we know what's in it. Being able to wield the sword is being able to use the truth of Scripture at any given point.

3. Authority (vs 18-24)

Now that we are ready for battle what happens next. We pray. Didn't completely expect that. Remember Christian warriors act differently in a war zone. This is a weapon no other army has available to them. This weapon brings forces that no enemy can defeat. Prayer is our war strategy. Constant communication with our commander in every season of conflict enables the believer to win the battles. To the Christian soldier, however, prayer is indispensable. Prayer crowns all efforts with success, and gives a victory when nothing else would. No matter how complete the armor, no matter how knowledgeable we may be in the study of war, no matter how courageous we may be, we may be certain that without prayer we shall be defeated. God alone can give the victory. When the Christian soldier goes forth armed completely for the spiritual conflict, if he looks to God by prayer, he may be confident of a triumph. This prayer is not to be intermitted. It is to be always. In every temptation and spiritual conflict we are to pray (Albert Barnes. Barnes NT Commentary). We must keep in constant contact with our commander to win the battle.

Prayer is for wartime, not for domestic convenience. We don't use it like we are calling our concierge for room service. We are calling down the power of the Holy Spirit in a war for the souls of men and women.

Paul "prayed in the spirit". This simply means we are so in tune with the Holy Spirit our desires are His desires. Our supreme objective is to glorify God; secondary is a blessing or request for us. The Holy Spirit guides our requests, and actually creates in us the faith that we need to see our prayer answered.

"When you cannot use your sword, and even when you can hardly grasp your shield, you can pray. That weapon of "all prayer" is of the handiest kind, because it can be turned in any and every direction." Charles Spurgeon

In verses 21-24, Paul encourages the Ephesian church by sending another believer, Tychicus, to them to strengthen them their faith. Paul sent someone he loved and trusted to encourage and continue to equip this church in Ephesus. Then Paul prays over them. He prays for peace during persecution, calm during a storm! He prayed that they would love with faith when you truly love someone you will believe the best! He concludes by asking God to bless the believers with grace, grace brings hope, strength, endurance and amazing inner peace.

Lessons Learned:

1. The greatest weapon a Christian can wield is how we live.
(1 John 2:6; Philippians 2:5; 2 Corinthians 3:16-18)

2. When at war I need to be acutely aware of where my strengths lie. Our strength is in being fully prepared, fully armed!
(Hebrews 12:11; 1 Peter 5:8; Mark 13:33- 37)

3. God will intervene if I am willing to intercede. There is no timetable on intercession.
(Psalm 46:1; Jeremiah 33:3; Isaiah 64:4)

Group Questions:

1. Putting on armor is proactive. Why is "standing," emphasized? (Philippians 4:1-9; 1 Corinthians 16:13; 2 Thessalonians 2:13-17; John 16:33)

2. Our 4 enemies are identified in v.12. Who are they? Where do they reside? How can we defeat them?
(2 Peter 2:4; 2 Corinthians 10:3-5 Ephesians 2:2; James 4:7; 1 John 4:4; 1 Thessalonians 5:17)

3. The helmet of salvation speaks to the great hope of heaven, a great victory day! But Satan loves to discourage us. What does the Bible say we should do in the face of discouragement?
(Hebrews 6:11-12; 2 Corinthians 10:5; Romans 12:2; 2 Corinthians 4:8-18)

4. When should we pray? What does it mean to pray in the spirit? What can we get from the command to be alert? Who should we pray for?
(Luke 18:1; Romans 8:26; 1 Corinthians 2:11; Nehemiah 4:9; I Chronicles 4:10; John 17:9,20; 1 Timothy 2:2-3)

Ravi Zacharias shares how: "At the historic Amsterdam Conference for Itinerant Evangelists in 1986, a renowned Korean speaker, Billy Kim, told the story of an American soldier hiding in a bunker during the Korean War. When his commander ordered him to rescue some of his fallen mates on the front lines, the soldier nodded his head, took a covert glance at his watch, stalled till his commanding officer was out of sight, and simply made no move. Several minutes went by, and a colleague reminded him of his rescue assignment. Again he looked at his watch and delayed. Finally, he leaped out of the bunker and fearlessly began carrying his compatriots to safety.

"At the end of the day, a friend asked him to explain his actions. The soldier said, 'I was afraid because I knew I was not ready to die. I waited until my fear would be overcome—remembering that at a certain time every hour my mother had said she would pray for me. Then I knew that no matter what awaited me, I could face it."

Notes

Shine

Bibliography

~Bibliography~

Ephesians 1:

1. **Doud, Warren.** "Ephesians: an expositional Bible Study." Gracenotes.info. https://www.gracenotes.info/ephesians/ephesians01.pdf (accessed August 30, 2017).

2. **"Hetty Green."** Wikipedia. August 25, 2017. https://en.wikipedia.org/wiki/Hetty_Green Accessed August 28, 2017.

3. **"Values.com."** Values.co. https://www.values.com/inspirational-quotes/6791-turn-your-face-to-the-sun-and-the-shadows-fall. Accessed August 1, 2017.

4. **"We Can Have as Much of God as We Want."** Bible.org. https://bible.org/illustration/we-can-have-much-god-we-want. July 25, 2017.

5. Wiersbe,Warren W. Be rich. Colorado Springs, CO: Cook Communications Ministries, 2004. 1937.

Ephesians 2:

1. **"The Gift of Peace."** Grace to You. August 18, 2016. https://www.gty.org/library/articles/P21/The-Gift-of-Peace. Accessed June 13, 2017.

2. **Exell, Joseph S.** The Biblical Illustrator: Ephesians, Philippians, Colossians. V19. Grand Rapids, MI: Baker Book House Publications. 1978. 122-228.

3. **Hughes, Kent. Ephesians:** The Mystery of the Body of Christ. Wheaton, IL: Crossway Publications. 1990. 63-102.

4. **Maclaren, Alexander.** Expositions of Holy Scripture: Ephesians. V 13. Grand Rapids, MI: Baker House Publications. 1982. 81-127

5. **Metts, Wally. Ephesians:** All this and Heaven, Too! Denver, CO: Accent-B/P Publications, Inc. 1980. 12-18.

Ephesians 3:

1. Macarthur, John. "Experiencing the Power of Christ" (Audio). Sermon. Grace Community Church, Panorama City, CA, September 5, 1993. Accessed on June 30, 2017. https://www.gty.org/library/sermons-library/80-121/experiencing-the-power-of-christ

2. Ortberg, John. Love Beyond Reason. Grand Rapids, MI: Zondervan Publications. 2001. 2.
3. **Weirsbe, 79-101.**

Ephesians 4:1-17:
1. **Billheimer, Paul E. Love Covers:** a Biblical Design for Unity in the Body of Christ. Fort Fort Washington, PA: CLC Publishers, 1983. 7.
2. **Cooper, David C.** Timeless Truths in Changing Times. Cleveland, TN: Pathway Press. 2007.
3. Ice Age. Directed by Chris Wedge. Los Angeles: 20th Century Fox Productions, 2002.
4. **Maclaren, 194-224.**
5. **Ndhlovu, John.** The Book of Ephesians, PDF. Johannesburg: Cosmo Baptist Church, 2014. 40-49.

Ephesians 4:17- 32:
1. **Barber, Wayne.** The John Ankerberg Show. "A Brand New Way- Part 1. June 2016. https://www.jashow.org/articles/bible/bible-studies/ephesians/ephesians-audio/ephesians-wayne-barber-eph-417-18-a-brand-new-way-part-1-audio/. Accessed August 23, 2017.
2. **Dexter, Jason.** "Ephesians 4:1732 Inductive Bible Study Notes, Cross References, Outline and Discussion Questions." Ephesians: 173-2 Inductive Bible Study. 2007. https;//www.calligraphyforgod.com/biblestudy/ephesians-4-1732.html. Accessed May 6, 2017.
3. **Kim, Peter and Patterson, James.** The Day America Told The Truth. Upper Saddle River, NJ: Prentice Hall Publishers. 1991. 45.
4. **Hughes, 137-151.**
5 **Lucado, Max. "Hope for the Hard Heart"**. Faith Gateway. March 17, 2014. https://www.faithgateway.com/hope-for-hard-heart/#.Wah5-VKZOT8. Accessed August 2, 2017.

Ephesians 5: 1-20:
1. Johnson, Dr. S. Lewis. "Christians's Use of the Tongue". http://sljinstitute.net/pauls-epistles/ephesians/christians-use-of-the-tongue/. Accessed August 15, 2017.
2. Kroll, Chana. "Irena Sendler: Rescuer of the Children of Warsaw." chabad.org. **https://www.chabad.org/thejewishwoman/article_cdo/aid/939081/jewish/irena-sendler.**
3. **Strauss, Lehman.** Devotional Studies in Galatians and Ephesians. Neptune, NJ: Loizeaux Brothers Publishing. 1969. 179-198.
4. **Sumner, Sarah. "Bridging the Ephesians 5 Divide."** Christianity Today VOL 49, no 10. (October 2005): 59.t
5. **Weirsbe, 133-157.**

Ephesians 5:21-6:9:

1. **Cole, Steven.** "Lesson 47: Submitting to One Another". bible.org. May 6, 2013. https://bible.org/seriespage/lesson-47-submitting-one-another-ephesians521. Accessed July 6, 2017.

2. **Metts,76-87.**

3. **Miller, Ken. "Redeemed Relationships"**, Vessels of Clay Blog, November 19, 2013. Accessed May 13, 2017. https://vesselsofclay.org/2013/11/19/ephesians521-69/.

4. **Sanna, Ellyn. "Christian Service."** in A Gentle Spirit. Edited by Ashleigh Bryce Clayton. Uhrichsville, OH: Barbour Press. 1999. Loc 2045. (Kindle Edition).

Ephesians 6:10-24:

1. **Innes, Richard. "A Wartime Prayer"**. ActsInternational. http://www.actsweb.org/articles/article.php?i=298&d=2&c=2. Accessed May 6, 2017. 1. Maclaren, 337398.

2. Strauss, 224-244.

3. Wiersbe, 175-185.

4. Wilhelmsson, Lars. "Spiritual Warfare". VitalChristianity.org. http://www.vitalchristianity.org/docs/Eph%206.13-17%20Spiritual%20Warfare%20Part%20III2.pdfW. Accessed May 9, 2017